Just a Moment

Kirby Peterson

BookLeaf Publishing

India | USA | UK

Presentation by *BookLeaf Publishing*

Web: www.bookleafpub.com

E-mail: info@bookleafpub.com

ISBN: 9789363316591

First edition 2024

ACKNOWLEDGEMENT

If it weren't for my ability to receive reprieve from work in the summer months, I doubt that this book would be possible. I am grateful for the mandatory self-care that is available to those of us who work so hard in education during the academic year. This time away from meetings, mayhem, monotony, and behavior modification is a welcome respite for the tireless educators who find it difficult to take time for ourselves.

PREFACE

These words were written in the sometimes restless and sometimes restful late spring and early summer of 2024. When words come and go like the midday heat. Sometimes words were easy to find, but more often they were not. A true artist never knows when the muses will find her. She just waits with baited breath hoping for inspiration to strike, or when she's fortunate, the motivation and her media (her tools for creation) arrive simultaneously!

Art, including poetry, is a spectrum and it can be difficult to predict just how it will manifest itself. We are all creative, finding our own place on the creativity spectrum. We create everyday, some consciously and all unconsciously.

I hope this compendium of characters, this litany of letters, this whirlwind of words sparks your imagination, awakens the muses at your side, and ignites your curiosity!

Assumptions and the donkey between us

Stay inside. Keep it all inside. Don't tell
anyone.
Keep your words to yourself.
Let resentment rise.

Don't tell me what you want.
Make me guess.
Build double the distress.
I cannot read your mind, can you?

Build sandcastles of wax and ask me why they
melt.

Whether the words are audible
or in our heads
the conversations continue,
so then why do we choose to
endure our bloody tongues?

We fill the empty space
between us
with nonsense.
We fall apart
when we lean

on our own
imagined understanding.

That's why I ask you
to step outside. Please
taste the waters, feel the breeze,
dance
with your shadows; I'll be right
here, counting steps with you.

This is how we fall
and get back up
again.

If you stay inside
I'm scared you'll
run and hide.
No, please dance
with your shadows.

Fall, and I will catch you
as I fall
and you catch me.

Trust, fall, trip, climb, rise,
and I will dance with you.

Am I Enough to hold space for?

Diversity means every color, all the stripes.
It's you and me and us.
Division means I leave you behind
for my own interests.

We fall for the fresh paint
but forget the box of crayons
contains us all.

When they come for you
why do I not feel the pain?
When their clubs and guns
are placed at the ready
why am I not your shield?

Are we all doomed to fall
to the trap of our own safety?
Why can I not leave myself
for you?

But after all, I don't have to
abandon myself to fully
see you,
do I?

A dormant revolution

They say we
all have a cult, we
just haven't
found it
yet.

I find myself
slipping back
into comfort -
sidestepping
complacency.

I find myself
escaping today
in pursuit of
who I am.

If I can dip
my toes into the waters
of intellectualism and
validation and I find them
hydrating some sense
of my self, is that
pealing back plastic
layers I've built up

over the years?

Or is it painting
plaster over plungingly
porous patches of
skin?

What ointment can
this man apply
that might loosen
the strings
that tie him together?

They say stand
for something
so I won't fall
for anything, but
everyone's grandstanding
makes a lonely world
feel so crowded.

Can I not
just sit under
the fig tree and
listen?
Can I not
just soak
everything in?
Must someone

always push me
toward proselytism
even if
that someone
is me?

Are we the intellects
sitting on
the ivory shores
of revolution?
Are we the precarious
and precious ones
laying comfortably
on the shoulders
of our forebears
while our progeny
run hopeless into
a future that isn't there?

Is this my cult?
Or could I be one
with imagined importance?
Am I seeking
to create a following?
a feedback loop?
a validation vortex?
an echo chamber
of only love?

Would that be so -

no!
I cannot let my
head inflate, I will not
give into the earth
dragon inside me.
I will light a match
and ignite the
vacuum between
my ears.

Destroy the
cult before the prophecy
is fulfilled.
Oscillate once more
to the other end
of me.

Crawl back
into myself
so the dragon
will not destroy
the world
it did not
create.

the DEvIl you know

There's a new way to keep us down -
though it's not new at all.
Fear the repercussions to our reputations.
Fear what we're becoming to the other
so we won't speak out.

It's a new way to divide and conquer,
a new iteration of segregation.

If we retreat to similarity
we maintain the status quo.

The voices in the cave are loud
but familiar. We can survive
where we've practiced the evacuation
route. How can we swim in
unknown waters?

Country Club or public park?

Is fear the origin of our separation? You push
me down or push me to the edge. I push
myself into the ghetto you built for me.

First it's normal,
then correct, if correct,
they say it must be moral -
and the congregations believe the moral is
synonymous with the religious,

but are only saints
on the VIP list?
If religion is the "saints only" club,
it sure seems like division is the goal.

electionS year

Such a profound wedge
was driven between
our shoulders,
and depending where
the hammering began
denotes the side
on which we stand.

I'll shove you into
broken frames, while
you squeeze me into
fitted sheets.

Neither practice smells
of human dignity,
but the puppets
pull our shortest strings:
anger, fear,

and maybe one day,
love.

I see you
on the other
side of the fence.

I hear your children
playing. Something
from within me
reaches out-
ward.

If I submit my Yes
as Yes,
and my No
as No,
might I
permit you
to do the same?

Like and Subside

All the people walking
en masse. The congregation
swiftly filtered through
double doors to mass.

"Blue!" cries one
in response to
their "Black!"

Shouts
drown any
hopes of conversation
in favor of
monologue
after
monologue
after
monologue.

Crowds in the
comments cut
through conversations
and leave no room
for new perspectives.

untethered Bruce

You stepped out
into the great unknown.
You walked
untethered, like a stitch
unsewn.
Your steps,
a movement
in a moment
in time.

Our history,
civilization,
all war and all peace,
a pale blue dot
swirling in the void,
the vast space
that holds us.

What holds us?
Who?

We're so quick
to pat
our own backs,
but we're minute,

less than a minute
in this dot's grand life.

Flowers rise and
toddlers fall. Will we
ever find a solid
purpose? Will faith
forever remain
our guide?

Is there more
beyond us?

And we're certain
there's so much
more. Will our five
senses ever reach
beyond the shore?

Will we fall before
we grow to know?

Will our
endless
hubristic
desires to rise,
to accomplish, and
to achieve
push us into

infinity?

Or will we
float away
untethered,
only
to become
unknown?

no strings attached

Do
I need a
caretaker?
Someone
to watch
over
me?

Am I
that sad,
that sorry,
that incapable,
of behaving
myself?

Or is
it a drill
sergeant
with a rigid
schedule for
me to follow?

I'm a mess
when I'm alone.
This distress
compresses in

and inflates out
like a balloon
floating gently
on a stream.

The short blades
of grass quickly
approach. Something
everyone just
glides right
through, but
my sensitive
skin
     pops!
revealing
every bit
of my insides.

And I am
destroyed,
devastated
from the
very sight.

Will I ever
find a way
to walk
through
unscathed?

just Today

Tomorrow is
an eternity
from today.

Yesterday is
already etched
in stone.

All I have is
just today.

If I try to run
I can't escape
me. If I hide
away in dreams,
something always
wakes me.

All I have is
just today.

I cannot shed
the skin
I'm wearing,
or leave

myself behind
to find me.

This everyday
condition
we're forced
to share in.

All we have is
just today.

"To love outside
there must be
a wellspring
within you," is
what they say.

Still all I have is
just today.

I can build
a fortress
or burn
a bridge,
but the
trojan horse
won't run
away.

For all I have is
just today.

I can climb
a beanstalk
to the heavens
or dig a grave
to sit in 'til I'm
gray,

but nothing here
will fade away,
for all I have is
just today.

I can reach
for contentment,
satisfaction,
and bliss,

but when
my arm returns
it crawls
into today.

pareidolia

Indeed it is
cold here in
your shadow.

The vacancy left
in your absence
of words
cuts a hole
in me I cannot
fill.

Did I bruise
you? Am I missing
something?

In the void
I fill us both
with useless
narrative. I tie
strings to things
that were never
meant to
connect.

I find loose

associations
in my search
for explanations.

The space between
your words creates
a chasm in my heart.

Don't you know
the length I go
for you? And me?
I leave me behind.

I starve myself
to feed your needs.

When we're apart
I consider every
thought, and when
you're near it's
alright.

When your
shoulder stares
me down, I crumble,
but how could I
tell you? You're so
fragile in such
a state, so volatile,

though never irate.

I asphyxiate as
you fixate but
all our words
evaporate.
You say it all as
you stare
to the side. Every
rational reason
fades
from my mind,
and the factitious
fictions fill every
formerly free
crevice.

Maybe I made it
all up in my mind.
Maybe I made you
make me
pause and rewind,
and rewind,
and rewind,
and see heartstrings
where anyone else
would be blind.

here today

The oldest buildings
were built to last.
The quick materials
fall so fast.

Were those before
more spiritual than us,
or were their gods
immune to rust?

We worship towers made
of money,
our egos, and accomplishments,
we bow down at the altars
of ourselves,
our leisure, and recreation.

When will we learn?

Our focus has become
nearsighted; the web
we've spun entangles
rather than embraces
us.

Our treasures rust,
and rot, and fade away.

We live so fast
that the sun consumes us,
and somehow
we still do not
understand the brevity
of our lives.

We live so fast and
fade so quickly, why
reinforce the bonds
that hold us
together
if we'll be
gone
tomorrow?

Why close
the window and
turn up the air?
Who could be
bothered? Why
do we care?
It's not our
future, not our
share. No, today
is our everyday
and tomorrow
might as well
not be there.

Scars and Gripes

Spinning at unimaginable speeds
and yet we do not stumble.
All the planets, every star and
satellite beyond us.

Everything a part of us, and our
monuments just collecting
stardust.

Are there truly invisible
strings between us? Do
each of us have
a hidden destiny?

Or perhaps it is
a collective conscious?
A web entangled
in each other's everything.

We get so caught
up in all our
stars and stripes,
czars and hype,
our
scars and gripes.

Whenever we near
our source,
the pendulum swings
and we're lost once
more,

but the tower
of Babel precedes
the upper room.

And the lonely
planet still
spins.

Run for (your) Office

Stand atop your tower
and gawk at us. Put us
in our place. Surely you
know us better than
we know ourselves.

Your satin sheets, your
velvet chair, your leather
boots, your slicked back
hair - you carry them
like badges.

What could we know
about our world? You
open your mouth
and poetry flows.
Titans bow before your
majesty. Surely,
there is no one
like you.

They say
the blind cannot
lead the blind, but
our ears are not deaf

to your lies. We hear
you when you say you see
us. We hear the whispers in
your chambers. You may fool
us for a moment, or maybe two
or three, but the light will always

find you.

Run, you exalted stain. Your
shadows cannot hold you.
Run with your buffered
posse, surely they
will protect you.
Run like you
did when

you begged for our vote.

Run like the wind, for
your time is shorter
than the hair
on the back
of your neck.

idolic guerrilla

You painted your life in rebellion
and a vision of a 21st Century man.
You fought and fought and fought
for the downtrodden and civically sick.

You left your homeland for revolution
only to have your lifeless body exploited
like a trophy.

You fought the greedy capitalist machine
and now he profits from your likeness.

You stood up straight and spoke directly
while so many others were content to
close their eyes, lay down, or bow.

Your enemies were many
and your methods unconventional,
and even though the machine
continues to profit from your
now lifeless likeness
you still stand
for revolution.

An ironic emblem,

a dynamic man diluted.
A sacrilegious saint,
a prophet not welcome
in his hometown.

Was there ever
a just assassin
or an honest statesman?
Was life stolen from
you? Was our world not
ready, or were you just
on time?

an inauguration of hope

The once oppressed cannot strip
themselves of the yoke of servitude
only to bind the next generation in their
ironclad chains of dependence.

The geopolitical world cannot
thrive in a game of whose hand is
on top. We cannot continue to
sleep while the tears of the
brokenhearted drown our debates
about which side has it best.

We cannot continue to live
in a dichotomous world if
we truly believe the visible
spectrum to be more than
black and white.

We must see our sister,
the widow, our brother,
the rebel, our father,
the learner, our mother,
the migrant, and ourselves
in the other.

We are not strangers in
this world. We are
one, though we are
many. We cannot forget
the master was
once the slave, the
statesman was
once an insurgent,
and the orphan was
once a precious child.

We all were once
precious children,
crying at the feet
of our mother.

If we are to seek liberty
for one, there can no longer
be any
one
oppressed.

We are they
who are oppressed.
They are us
who are without
an advocate.

We are the pushed aside,

the ignored, the abused,
oppressed, and forgotten.

They are us and we are
them, there is no division.

memento mori

There is no magic pill,
no silver bullet,
no sudden savior.

The love potion is
just perfume,
the snake oil
only venom.

All the remedies
you seek in life are just
temporary balm
or early embalming oil.

The moment you take
your first breath
the embalming oil
is removed from its shelf.

Death is not a foe
to fear, or a thief set on
stealing you,
but a stranger
to befriend, so fear
not the end.

the Rhythm of nowhere

Sitting down to escape
the everything
of somewhere,
settling in to
the rhythm
of nowhere.

Suddenly noticing
the swirling clouds,
the shivering trees,

everything swaying
around me
to the same rhythm
of the cells
within me.

I am not Saturn,
these woods are
not my dusty rings.

This setting is
our universe - galaxies
upon galaxies
of rocks and stars, all

dancing in step
with each other.

These mountains are
never isolated,
the range is
a family
among families - never
competing, just living
in their relative
company, each peak held
by the next generation.

two is one

I am not
my brother's keeper.
I am
my brother
and
my brother
is me.

I see his face
in the mirror
and he hears my
thoughts
between his ears.

He falls and
I get back
up.

No Escape

If I never
fall
I can never
rise.
If I lay
in wait
there is no guarantee
of returning.

Alone,

enforced or voluntary,
        is a death sentence.

It may be
true
that many
a desire is

solitary,

but when
we're truly

alone

for days
        and years
                and ages,

Death
will ultimately knock
down our door.

previous peaks

Depression contains
such slippery sidelines.
It's hard to describe
to those living beyond
the bylines.

A week can peak and
the plateau can feel so
shallow, so hollow, so
empty or removed of all
previous life.

Depression takes over
despite the lack of
an invitation.

"Just take
your medicine." "Pull
yourself together." "Talk
to the One."

Everyone has
an opinion, an answer,
a regimen, a solution.

Some have sympathy,

fewer have empathy.
Some hear,
fewer listen.

Some seek to solve, and
somehow those
who do not
end up with
the solution.

Catharsis creeps around
precarious corners
and seldom stays in
the same space twice.

Sleep is sometimes
solace, but
rest is mostly
restless.

Art becomes
an avenue,
poetry a project,
and somehow they
change places, project-
ing something from
nothing and filling blanks
that are better
left empty.

www.ingramcontent.com/pod-product-compliance
Lightning Source LLC
LaVergne TN
LVHW021303200726
843509LV00012B/1754